A HOTEL
LOBBY
AT THE
EDGE
OF THE
WORLD

Also by Adam Clay
The Wash (Parlor Press, 2006)

A HOTEL LOBBY AT THE EDGE OF THE WORLD

ADAM CLAY

milkweed
editions

Milkweed Editions, 1011 Washington Avenue South, Suite 300,
Minneapolis, Minnesota 55415.
(800) 520-6455
www.milkweed.org

Published 2012 by Milkweed Editions
Printed in the United States
Cover design by Hopkins/Baumann
Interior design by Hopkins/Baumann
Cover photo © iStockphoto.com/icetraystanislav
Author photo by Kimberley Clay
The text of this book is set in Bodoni.

12 13 14 15 16   5 4 3 2
First Edition

Please turn to the back of this book for a list of
the sustaining funders of Milkweed Editions.

Library of Congress Cataloging-in-Publication Data

Clay, Adam, 1978-
    A hotel lobby at the edge of the world : poems / Adam Clay. -- 1st ed.
        p. cm.
    ISBN 978-1-57131-441-3 (acid-free paper)
    I. Title.
    PS3603.L385H68 2012
    811'.6--dc23
                                    2011029979

This book is printed on acid-free paper.

for P, before we even knew you

Contents

II.

III.

IV.

Acknowledgments

Earlier versions of these poems appeared in the following journals:

751 Magazine — "Maybe Motion Will Save Us All" and "Myth Left in Memory"
A Public Space — "Thought For a Stalled World"
Barn Owl Review — "For the Driftwood I Once Loved" and
       "Scientific Method"
Bat City Review — "[Seven years into the longest],"
       "[A shadow glimpsed inside]," and "[But a thought always hinges]"
Boston Review — "Goodbye to All That, the Birds Included"
Cannibal — "Poem in Place of a Fractured Sonnet"
Court Green — "Natural History"
Diagram — "In Light of Recent Developments"
Gulf Coast — "Sonnet"
Horse Less Review — "Slow Dancing Around What I Really Have to Say"
La Fovea — "Self-Portrait with House Slippers and Tap Water"
The Laurel Review — "Recalling an Earlier Snow During a Present Storm"
       and "Song"
Mantis — "Gathered" and "Harbor"
New Orleans Review — "Poem Beginning with a Line from Tranströmer"
Ninth Letter — "What Movement Sounds Like"
Octopus Magazine — "I'm Pretty Sure That's a Hurdle in the Distance"
Parthenon West Review — "A Thought Before Thought"
Phoebe — "Reaching for a Lexicon, an Apple No Longer Shining"
Strange New Egg — "Fragment for an Avoided Disaster" and
       "Slow Dancing Around What I Really Have to Say"
Sycamore Review — "The Last Horse"
The Tusculum Review — "Light Bulb Hum" and "Vine"

"As Complete as a Thought Can Be" appeared as a hand-sewn limited
edition chapbook from Cannibal Books. Thank you to Katy and Matthew Henriksen.

Thank you, also, to Alex Lemon, Wayne Miller, Michael Robins,
Kate and Max Greenstreet, James Cihlar, Shannon Jonas, Zachary Schomburg,
Matt Hart, Nancy Eimers, William Olsen, and Kimberley Clay.

A HOTEL LOBBY AT THE EDGE OF THE WORLD

Scientific Method

Twenty-three percent when placed under
intense pressure did in fact kick
the door in. Soldiers creep on the other side
of the turn. Every little thing
is destined for ease. Music, be still.

Keep the mannequin secrets
to yourself. Remember a ladder
can take you both up and down.
The weather grows less stable
than us. This line here is where

the season starts. Spring seems
fluorescently golden. Too much
milk in the fridge. When left alone
long enough, the prisoners
began to interrogate themselves.

I

You exist only in the
delirious illusion of language.

– Robert Penn Warren,
"Brotherhood in Pain"

Natural History

What we think of as Natural History
exists quietly in the oldest elevator this side

of the Mississippi. A town built on hills —
and then, southbound.

Centering yourself along unrecorded boundaries,
it's only when you come upon
a creek in the woods that the concept of remoteness

      dawns on you

            as something more than distance.

The tree is a metaphor for something, as is the creek, as is your sightline.

      You value landscape for the way it is both certain and changing.
         You value a boat for the same reason.

      How many boats are waiting here in the forest?

         The lyric quality of a weed. Air's rapture near noon.

And then noon.

      And you cannot think of a prayer even if it means the difference
         between being saved and being damned.

      Nothing here has a name.

The tree is a metaphor for something, as is the creek, as is your sightline —

I'm Pretty Sure That's a Hurdle in the Distance

I could have run from repetition
forever. Dearest sun, your thick light

drags me down like a river current —
a big river, a small current. Anything

I say could start with repetition
and end with light. A shortcut to save

breath. Breathing. Light. Newsprint-
smudged forehead. Four-of-a-kind.

Where the hills rose up, people
grew really tired and settled. This is

easy to understand. A head filled
with vowels in a consonant world.

I'm fairly sure you could finish
my sentences and make them better.

What else did you think
a question was designed for?

Sonnet

I am trying to find a line of tenderness
to walk tonight. But wishing for something —
a deer, a possum, a squirrel, anything —
to make its way across the boulevard
at this moment would suit me fine. Do we wish
for words and then they come to us? Do we wish
for words and say the opposite of what we mean?
Syntax has never eaten from my hand. One night,
I gnawed a bone long after the wine was gone,
and you picked the cork down to nothing.
You drove, reached to shift gears,
remembered the car was an automatic.
I would not and will not touch you
before we find a word to settle between us.

Slow Dancing Around What I Really Have to Say

A quiet sky crowded
above houses, crowded

together too. Bones
are breaking all over

the Midwest at this very
moment and we listen

and we move in
and hush

the neighbor dog
and hush our breathing

and hear nothing.
The South Shore Line

does its job,
curves around the lake

and Up North there
is water everywhere,

the sky glows red
like a firework out

of touch with the air.
Always I have wanted

to say how symmetrical
everything is — that is if you

stare at it long enough.

Fragment for an Avoided Disaster

My mind re-imagining the glass
I drank from then,

just so I can break it.
The doctors call this re-visionary.

A person can leave a loaf
of bread in a field.

What happens next is out
of his or her hands.

I did not break the glass that night
in New England and now, years later,

I cannot begin to express my regret.
Several times I have thought

it was five years earlier when it was not.

Poem Beginning with a Line from Tranströmer

Here I come, the invisible man, perhaps employed
by something only the dead
can articulate in their oily view of the past
and their eagerness for a future, a future
they have forgotten even exists.
Here I go, lost in a game of chess

with weather, a game of latitude
with the mast of a ship,
a game of searching gone black
by night. What I desire in the sleepy
folds of repetition — only a crumb.
May I for a moment be nervous

breath beneath the sky's slivered
blue? As if offered an excuse to turn
my back on the horizon,
I am only a crow holding
my flight pattern, turning away
from violence and other kinds of weather.

The Last Bread Crust

A mixing of the senses,
three dollars in your pocket,
and the month-long storm:
rain, the most beautiful
iambic pentameter in the world.
Someone said the rain
would mean nothing
if thirst had never been named.
Maybe I'm just replaying
the conversation about
the eternal selfishness
of nature, everything crowding
around the last bread crust
on Earth. You are in a cage
ten feet above. The days go on
for months and months,
the bread crust rotting,
and nature still acts
as though it does not see you.

Self-Portrait with House Slippers and Tap Water

— after Jay Hopler

1.

      In bed — a rose thorn

in my finger. A celebration
of the day was all I turned out to be.

2.

Maybe *disappearing* is what I meant.

A lover's hair clogging the drain —

maybe *disappearing* is what I meant?

3.

The beginning of a beautiful season!

4.

Even if what they say—*pain exists
to magnify love* —
were true,
you wouldn't change your hum
to accommodate loneliness.

5.

O dog, O dog, can I understand hunger
for a moment
through your mind?

What would heaven be
if you couldn't manage abstractions?

6.

Or if you could?

7.

Headlights for a reading lamp —
The beginning of a beautiful season —

8.

I am washing the sand,
I am washing each grain of sand.

The Last Horse

There is no street as narrow as this one.

I held a brick up to block the sky,
but it remained nothing more
than the sum of its dust. One summer
I counted these bricks — the space between
them seemed more defined and less blurred
by the sun — it took all summer.

Each star in the sky matched up to a single brick,
all of them all threaded together —
as in Giotto's *Receiving the Stigmata*
when St. Francis realizes
literally nothing separates
him from the heavens.
I realized each star in the sky was a divine
brick. That perfect laugh rising
from the corner of the decaying
neighborhood bar remained holy as well.

Everything was, and everything wasn't —
this lesson was more difficult than the first one.
How desperate the light from the factory was.
How desperate I was to perceive something sacred
in the heavy air drifting up and out and away.

But there was nothing holy about the intangible.
There was only the last horse.
After it was gone, the imprint on the bricks
remained. Then the memory of the horse.
Then rain for a thousand years.

On the Momentum of Memory

Where a vine is only a vine,
where two sparrows flying fast
around the house, not expecting
to find me standing here,
are just what they appear to be:
two sparrows lost for half
a second in my shadow.
Dreaming of momentum.
Dreaming of five minutes
along this path of weeds and ticks
to recall a memory that might
have avoided resurrection
for too long. From one iniquity
to the next. A blur of a triptych
I saw years ago. The sky:
the grainy texture of gravel.
What will survive of us
is not love but rather water
and sound and light.
The museums will it so.

For Your Eyelash Anchored to the Sky

I am riding backward through Michigan toward Chicago.

I am thinking of a specific place in time.

A smashed caterpillar somehow on a windshield.

Somehow, otherhow.

I am always wishing you were here.

I am thinking of a general place in time.

I was watching a boot fill up with blood — and I said nothing.

A school of geese: each one turns to a door when I touch your hand.

What can we say to the inside of a piano?

Can you play it with your teeth?

I am tying a typewriter to my leg with a heavy piece of thread.

Because I do not want to be dragged to the bottom.

Because I want to watch thousands of words spill out and up toward me.

I want to watch you laughing down from the pier.

I want to breathe fire only to see my reflection in your iris.

Your left iris. The one sculpted from a thousand tiny feathers.

Poem in Place of a Fractured Sonnet

I went fishing north of here and said a prayer for no one. As I waded,
      midnight destroyed what reservations I had about the water.

               In winter
          this river mostly freezes over,

      but at that moment it was August and still warm. Glacial
      outwash made up most of the soil.

So I thought
          about this fact
for a while, but it didn't take me back to an age
      of ice like I had hoped.

             It just made me shiver and move forward.
     I do a lot of moving forward while thinking
          about the past and the weather thousands

     of years ago in the very place
I'm moving forward while standing still.

     I could take you to the place
where I had my hair cut each month for five years.

I could take you to the place
          where the dogs walk on their hind legs.

But I won't.
          What I'll tell you is that I stood

in the river until it froze over. I was wistful when the sun set
each night but not for what had happened to me,

          to us, but for what was yet to happen.
                    Completely without pessimism,
          I knew what could happen

and knew I was nowhere near prepared for it, yet
I slipped under the water as though

          it could somehow — as though
it could even ready me for its song.

Song

Where did I leave my
Where did I leave my projection, my ashen skin, my rhyme,

    My cast-iron skillet in the coals?

Let me think category   without meaning anything
Let me think noise   without meaning camera angle

Stumble over a comma? Dear,
    Let's stumble over disaster like it's normal

Because it is,   I am
Disaster summarized

Dear —
I am a line from Whitman knotted in itself

Untie the sky
Think of me in the act

II

Harbor

The ice machine in the hallway
Hummed a medicated noise
But we heard a song
Checked into the hotel
Left the lights off for the night
Watched the TV in the room
Across the street
Through a window
In another hotel
And bore with discipline
What we saw there —

A mountain pine beetle found alive in an oak

As Complete as a Thought Can Be

1.

Seven years into the longest
century. How many light bulbs
burnt out, how many mornings
did I wake to a clattering
kitchen, the heat pushing
through the roof of the house,
out into the atmosphere
as it pressed downward? I am only
starting to gather up what
I claim as my own. Waiting
for someone to call me out,
I am amazed at how many
days can go by in which I say
nothing. A brick wall is only
a brick wall until you pull
a brick out and watch
the whole thing fall. When I think
of metaphor, the last thing
to enter my mind is a brick wall.
It falls — like a tree — slowly
and silently until the pavement
bears its weight and it becomes
something altogether different.

2.

A shadow glimpsed inside
a building just before
it was imploded, recorded
by an amateur. The amateur,
too, had showered that morning
and thought of barbed wire
and a pair of nail clippers
dropped out of a moving
car, sparking the sidewalk.
Sometimes reading the news
over coffee, I am suddenly
overjoyed — though
I know I should not be,
with so many bombs
in the world, so many
bombs going off, I mean,
but at this desk the snow
slows down just enough
for me to see through it. A roof
pitched this way. A song
too. I keep expecting
the frame of every building
I enter to give way. Once
on the South Shore Line
we passed a farm with
a dozen hay bales and one
was on fire and we could
smell the smoke inside
the car and everyone
looked and then looked glad
to be moving on.

3.

But a thought always hinges
on another. But I think
of news and noise
as one thing: static
sticking to my coat-sleeves.
I gave myself over
to the ocean
once and it spit me
back out onto the sand,
turned me into a bark
from the dog next door.
Deep into winter
the smell of salt stronger
and stronger. Then we
are not old. Then we are
born again and we
are taking the bread
and slipping it into
our palms giving
it to the people
on the street as though
the people there will know
what to do with it; and
sometimes sometimes
I see you and sit
next to you and one time
I did not even know
how to begin speaking
or even hoping
for an earthquake
or even hoping and
knowing I might
find out what
I was supposed to say.

4.

Because noise is never
born to be itself,
we now hear someone trying
to turn the back doorknob,
trying to open our house
up to the world, to make
the house a part of it, to make
the house a frame, a place where
something happens. Because
we grow younger
in our sleep. Because we drive
around looking for a good place
to catch a fish. Because cans
float upstream and history
is not always doomed to repeat
its record-skipping: learn it
or refuse to. Because I am
starting to sound like a voice
that once haunted
my sleep, I will parallel park
in my first attempt and step
outside of the car and cram
each and every laugh
into the storm sewer and roll
up my sleeves tonight
and know what I am capable of
and then wish and wish we were
born at the same time and wish
that we had not missed a single
moment of one another.

5.

Arc of dust, archipelago-like.
Beside the sink
an altar of dirty dishes
and newspapers
and newspapers
with the ink rubbed off,
with the world outside rubbed
off. Step outside and see
the burning pile
of leaves, watch a brick
being made and think
of rust on a handrail
and a handrail leading
nowhere and a handrail
going somewhere,
somewhere: standing on
a peninsula and swearing
you saw a sun but it
was only a tree burning
color into the sky.

6.

Jonah looked into
the whale and saw
a building falling
all around him and
the world did not
exist until that moment
when Jonah looked into
the whale and saw
a building falling
all around him.

7.

Not for a lack
of understanding
but for a lack
of understanding
maps, I found myself
lost in the big
city and finding
my way by airplanes
cutting across
building tops as if
the hills were just
on the other side
of the city and
they *were* eventually,
though I swam
in the river first
and walked
through a mirror
too. What I left
in the mirror,
what I left in the net
below the tightrope
walker, was the hum
that victims of
lightning strikes
say they hear right
before and then
forever after.

8.

We sat by the lake
and watched the swans
glide in and thought
we might be older
than we were, but I only
had a single gray hair
and you weren't old
either, yet the swans
were still beautiful
and the glow around
the day did not dull
for quite some time
after that. If I were
interested in the idealistic,
I'd say there was a picnic
basket and a bear
in the brush watching
us, the swans, the picnic.
But there were no bears
that near the city
and the Midwest was strange
and it's even stranger
here with the turkey buzzards all
lined up on a single telephone line
above the park. We walked
in a circle for a few hours
after all of that bird-
watching and I am glad
for snow in the summer-
time. I am glad you always
answer the phone when I call.

9.

Always in anticipation of
noise in the morning
as though something
might wake me from
sleep, something violent
might stir me, might make
the crick in my neck
creak away into the corner
of the house that still
is somehow undiscovered,
the place where a lack of
belonging feels right at home.
At two a.m. I was shuffling
the flour and the sugar
and the rice tins in the kitchen,
and I thought of what
a kitchen could look like
with you in it at that moment,
and it made me nostalgic.
What I thought I was able
to do was impossible.
Even parallel parking
had become tedious.
If I dream about dreaming
one more time, I will dream
myself into a tiny room,
and the spoons in my pocket
— the ones carefully stowed
away — will not even
allow me to escape.

10.

A state out of state
out of hours
to think silently to myself,
to bridge back into something
unsure and uncertain, field-
dressing a wound but the infection
out here is infectious
like no other. Home
late home, always late,
like fire burning
down a house and you're coming
around the corner to see a
pile of ash, a pile of wind
blows ash in your eyes, ask what
the wind can do if it can blow the ash
back into the shape of a house,
and if the wind can be only the wind
in a poem where you are standing
alone, and the wind pulls itself
together, and you are glad to be bold
and glad to be laughing
at the memory of a moment.

11.

The world slants toward
a drain in the ground
and, if you're doubting,
do as I do: prick a finger
and let the blood drop
to the floor in the center
of any room.
How many drops?
How many times in the face
of a mirror have I said these words,
simplistically, before
turning the light bulb
to turn out the light?
This morning I swept
the leaves off the front
porch onto the sidewalk
and heard someone
ten streets over
walking home from the bars,
hair standing straight up
on my arms, and the teardrop
streetlight hummed itself back to life,
it hummed itself to life again,
and I thought of a saint
whose purpose it would be
to see us home at night,
to send us home with a broom
in hand, with a flickering
streetlight to guide us home.

12.

Sometimes when I think *you*
I am thinking *I,*
and this might be
enough explanation
for right now. Most of what
you see
you see
through a camera lens
first. And if the lens cap
stays on, then so be it,
you have to sleep, we all
have to sleep, and we all
have to process and organize
and reorganize. You
think image, you
think five hundred. A card
catalogue when you were
a child, and when you were
a child the sound of the card
catalogue drawer opening and
closing, and you put whatever
it was back in there, and you ignored
the sky looking down at you.

13.

What can we think of history
if we are thirsty above all
else? And what if I am
the only person in Michigan,
snow shovel in hand,
looking toward the sky
at this moment? If
a brick can turn cold,
then I can turn cold.
If a wheelbarrow can
stay outside, I can
stay outside and think
of history and how passive
history can be in the glare
of a face staring back at it.
I want to parallel park
for five years straight. I want
to pardon some felons
and laugh into the table-
cloth, and let the laugh
carry itself under the table.

14.

A clock wound tight,
tight-wound clock.
Gather round the fire.
I am disregarding present
company more and more
these days. I am making
the sky more and more
an envelope that need
not hold anything. And inside,
away from the rain, inside,
the news blares blue and blares,
and if you look into
any drink in your hand
and don't see yourself,
then don't drink it. Don't
think you can see
your face in every single
cloud. Clouds are different
than water and a mountain
takes you closer and farther
away. I am beginning
to think a fragment
is as complete as a thought can be.

15.

Sit across a desk from the sun
and answer its questions, its
one question, rather. Go someplace
and come back and there the sun
will be waiting for its answer,
its answers. I am certainly tired
of certainty and hoping for a herd
of cows to cross the road
each time I try to leave town,
and each time I come back home,
the plastic bags rattling around
in the back of the car, the groceries
growing warm in the sun. What
can you do with a chalkboard
if you have no chalk? Scan
the horizon for an exit
that might take you
somewhere. Glance through
the newspaper for something
you might have said
without even thinking it.

16.

And someone said
we are only the language
we speak, nothing more.
A splice of light
can fall across my eyes
and a splice of light can softly
catch a radio wave and make
me think of a world incinerated
to dust. We are the words,
yes, but we are swallowing
swords by the second, by
the handful. What I meant
to say, I said, I think
and I've glanced up at the TV
again and again as if I might
see something in it I have not
seen before. It's off, you tell me,
it's off, I know, but there are at least
five thousand stories in the dust,
in the small talk of dirt. A dam
of light in the river of night:
watch the headlights swerve
into a tree like it was always
meant to happen.

17.

It's amazing that we are here.
I'm sure the papers
would beg to differ. I'm sure
that if you cut today's paper
into a dozen paper dolls
they would become
something greater than the sum
of their parts. Language is the center
of their being, of course, but I am
sure that when my voice cracks it is honesty
in its purest form, and loneliness
is at the back door,
just out of sight from the streetlamp's
light. A long line of people
somewhere stretches around
a block, and the people wait to eat.
The people wait for bread in their
hands and if this country wasn't
the country where I was born,
I'd swear my stomach would growl
and I would ask you, plead with you,
for a caption, a footnote —
for the place where this photograph
was taken to be placed in
someone's pocket and turn
the tint of mustard gas.

18.

And then snow — the sky turns
orange, the Saint of Snow Blowers
finds an apple in the gutter: the way
we think love should be, the way we think
love is. In a dream I answered a ringing phone —
there was a fire on the other end — somehow
I just knew — yet I had to answer. Stringing
silence into the mouth of a fire is like
talking to yourself in the hours before
anyone else in the world is awake or alive
and what you say depends not on rhetoric
but on the temperature of the receiver.
The news becomes a soundtrack playing
behind my voice when I speak: a bed
of coals we walk across to understand
the limits of flesh. Some mornings I don't
even answer the phone. Some mornings I
repeat a thought the way I repeat a breath.

19.

In anticipation of a fragment breaking down
in anticipation of a fragment breaking down

in anticipation of a fragment breaking down
in anticipation of a fragment breaking down

in anticipation of a fragment breaking down
a child draws a line. A constellation
creaks closer
toward a half-moon,
a half-moon that is unchanging
and as constant as that line,
as if the child was aware — or already
in anticipation of a fragment breaking down.

20.

Setting up camp inside a heart:
a tent stake, a bit of brick
fleck in my eye. What a blink can
take away, what a shutter falling down
and lifting up can do to vision. A series
of parallel lines to the lake, crossing
more parallel lines, the sun glistening
like a flask in a field — it catches
my eye and lives there. Forgiven for
revealing so much about sight:
it seeks out a road and what seeks a road
must seek out some trees, some plants,
some snow for drinking water since
the fuel light is glowing — like a sun too —
and soon there are a million lights
and I am looking at myself
looking up at a tree of light.

III

Complaint's a sort of orchard.

–Graham Foust,
"Panama"

Recalling an Earlier Snow During a Present Storm

A tiny bit of wind meant for a tiny bit of landscape —
        and the grass is gone. Candy wrappers mixed in with the leaves,

sleight of hand somehow
        dangerous. Somehow, magic.

                Somehow asking for something,
and the flicker of the television downstairs on the timer

        set to go off at the same time every night
now does. And the world creaks by. And the house

                is quiet now that the television
        is off. And now that momentum and all of the other things

in the world that cannot be classified as movement
        are happening elsewhere,
                I can congratulate the night for bringing me here.

        And what we lose in defending nothing
                is something I'd like to lose myself in. Sometimes

        a tree blocks off the end of one street,
                but never the other end
at the same time. Ice makes most things heavier. Ice makes most things

        heave and break. The first snow
always sets me down somewhere else.

Thought For a Stalled World

In early June, a late frost, an airplane coming apart above us
        and then catching hold in the mind,
the dogs down the street lunging at each other,

        and the grass in your hair from yesterday:
still there. We have danced over, lived with, and barely missed
                countless splinters, except for the one
        that went right under my fingernail,

straight to the cuticle, a reminder that pain has a beauty
                all its own. The nail divided down the middle,
        a line drawn, an elegy hidden in each fingertip,
                an elegy slipping out in the middle of the night

        like it owns the place. Because it does. Because it does,
we put a price on beauty, on pain, on elegy,
        and think nothing of it. I do not wish to be didactic.

                I do not wish to preach to the boy
pulling his wagon down the cracked sidewalk,
                        the wagon missing a wheel,
                for he already knows as well as I do

that time is a pitchfork stuck sideways in a barn wall,
        a note pinned underneath reading

                "When Winds take Forests in their Paws
                The Universe — is still — "

        and even if it wasn't,
we wouldn't even know it. If moving feels

this way, think of what being still will do. Imagine
        thinking of beauty with no momentum behind it.

A Memory, Forgotten at the End of a Season

The light gives itself over to the storm
        and the train that runs through town —

the one you set your watch by —

            does not reveal
that you are filled with the need
        to document something,

as if the act of documentation will assure you
            that you exist. You hear the birds swarming,

      you hear the birds flapping their wings
just to stay alive. I know their colors from their song
        but not their names.
    You know the names.

        You know the day in late winter
when they trickle back through town. It is foolish
        to predict anything. It is foolish to predict the weather,

        which isn't anything that can be held —
        but still you try to hold it, stubbornly silent,

a hand upside down and a single bird last winter *(remember?*
    remember?) that flew in through

        the open door, the one that right now,
as far as we can tell,
      still waits in the attic dreaming of flight.

For the Driftwood I Once Loved

I do not know what voice I am hearing right now.

When I think of voice, it is the South
I think of again and again, and how the South shed

its rustic laugh for a noble one, how it shed its laugh for streetcar
    sounds and Memphis weeds in an Arkansas field.

            Downward sloping sidewalk. Hesitation wounds
in the sky. A crabapple for each one. A cherry blossom

        in her teeth. I am listening to my throat click. I am hearing
                a ghost long gone.
            Marble eyes I had never seen before,
                    all weather I wish to tie a neat ribbon around.

        A meaningful piece of fabric. A sigh.
                Sometimes I do not know what direction

    the East is, especially at dusk. The mosquitoes are drunk
            with the love we have left in our veins.
I want to tell each of them a story. I want to recreate whatever

        it was I forgot. Once, far from here, at the Haymarket
            in Boston, I realized
                I didn't know the woman

            I was there with — that not even her hand in mine
        felt real, that the smell
of rotting fruit and fish might have stirred me,
            might have woken me up —

        but instead the sky folded in on itself,
        and I kept sleeping, kept waiting for it to open back up.

Myth Left in Memory

—*for Mathias Svalina*

Five thousand dreams of a city. An oar pointed
    parallel to the sky. An oar in a dream
        urges sleep forward. Always fleeing

    something,
I am a part of night, a part of a conversation
    that gazes a bit to the left.

        What the stars say. Always fleeing something.
The stars lift nothing nearer to them,

        as if animation is a gift they can offer. As if a gift
    they can offer would even be a gift. A sightless god
suspended in a cage looks to water
    for his reflection. An oar disrupts the water,

    turns this creation myth
on its head, pushes the blank-faced narrative toward the river,
turns it over, sends it

    back out again. What is worthwhile? A narrative
        such as this, tied into something greater?
    A narrative such as this, tied into itself,

might bring the head
    of salvation on a platter. There is a briny taste
    in my mouth. There are ten thousand years of salt in the air around
me. Around me, there is enough light

    to see my hands at work, to see the tiny waves born from silence
    facing in the direction someone once dreamt up.

What I once thought I knew has turned to noise and light.

A Thought Before Thought

whether I can prove it or not
—William Olsen

It would be a lie to say
        there is no desire whatsoever to return

to that place, that moment, where light
        first touched my skin, swaddled

        outside of a hospital or in the back seat
        of a car on the freeway, the dull

orange light of the defroster
filling the car as if it was the first light

        in the world. Job cursed that light
saying *Let darkness and the shadow of death stain*

that day, as if a stain could join it
        to a world gone wrong.

I said all of these things — and more — to a river
        where all of the fish

had become female, where a heron
        did not turn its head to look at me.

For the Earnest Days Before Summer

When a breeze gives you a chair to sit in.
    When a baby crawls toward you.

When the memory of your discovery
    of North America becomes more like a dream

than reality — your feet
    on the sand, salt in your mouth,

        a thousand flies swarming your face,
another thousand flies swarming your face,

    you remember
what you had meant to forget:

      Look at a leaf and see your face.
    Look at *the sound of one hand clapping* and hear it forever.

Look to the noise of a newspaper in the wind
    and hear it become the wind —

    O the wind, a nursery of babies screaming for you,
      one of them is yours, but the others

are only hungry, dear soul, dearest
    dark. Damaged noise in your mind.

      When. When you think of the dark.
When you think what you think you are. When it engulfs you.

When the television blares and you don't hear it.
When a hay bale rings on the nightstand
and you answer it.

(If it rings, answer it.)

When you find your voice.
When you light a cigarette
for the dead smoker on the other end. Wind.

When you reinvent grammar,

and that new grammar hems you in.

When every thought of a situation
is plagiarized from Audubon, unintentionally,
a dream on the edge of a field

in the mind of America.
Focused. Distracted.

The corn circled around the city. A flag
for every leaf on every tree. A revival

of silence. A cup of coffee
for every morning. A martyr for every ocean. Telemachus
among a thousand others.

A martyr on fire inside every recorded explosion.

Vine

Digital wolves are chasing a digital horse on the television,
                and the streets of Kalamazoo are quiet

        for the first time in months.
    It is not snowing. It is not what I envisioned.

Some of the wolves are kicked
            off their feet and die. The mosquitoes outside

        turn blue
in the streetlights coming on, the glare of some unknown lake

        terrifies even the fish.
           What can I say

        in the wake of a season torn in two, in the wake of a storm
           someone a few houses down

said would come through town and pile house upon house,
           as if justice were somehow submerged in the rain
    and the wind?

        As if justice can make any of us feel less alone —
I am not listening. I am not

        climbing down from this tree
        just to see how the grass feels under my feet.

What Movement Sounds Like

Asleep fast, always. Fast asleep. A clinging ghost, ashy, cold,
    the house creaks
        as if dropped in water and sinking still. Chalk lines

above us from three F-16s,
    only it's dark and they cannot be seen — the pilots

recline further into night. The language of transportation is a noise
        outside our window — a train headed for Chicago

    can take your breath away if you stand by the tracks —
        but if you are sleeping, its whistle
    is only catalogued with the chalk lines

and the thump of a stereo stuck inside a closed window. If I hold
    my hands open to catch movement, I go nowhere.

    One morning before the sun rose,
I went out to shovel the snow and saw Pearl,

        ninety-six, hunched with an ice pick chipping
away at the drive, filling the space between the houses with clatter,

    while her body was buried
        elsewhere. We wake to keep from being still.

A Day in August

I sat for hours in the same seat in my favorite Chinese restaurant

      wondering what moderation could possibly mean
           in a place like this, in a world that gives

itself to you on a platter every night if you ask with the right tone
           of voice, if you sigh

      instead of breathe, if you sit still and give the impression
that you were always
           meant to fill that very space.

      There are a million excuses to be in transit. Just earlier today

I was sitting on the porch
           when a tree limb fell only seconds after my neighbor

was standing in the very place it landed. It was a big limb,
           not one I'd ever really noticed,

but when it fell, it gave the impression
that it might have
            brought blood to the surface. My neighbors are pretty much

            the opposite of me.

They spend most of their waking hours
            moving, and I spend most of mine

watching them go places. Often I want to follow them

            at a distance just to find where they go
or what it is they're looking for.

            Today they are loading up their car
and moving to the east side of town. I hope they settle down.
            I hope they get tired of

            moving.
Today, I am growing tired of the sun,

                        which is just beyond those clouds
behind those trees. Today I am hungry,
            and I don't think this feeling will ever go away.

Gathered

A Collage of Several Cities in Mid-America, 2003 – 2007

1.

A heroic couplet
                    in an un-heroic time:

drinking beer out of cans in suburban Cincinnati,
            the woods curled up around us,

the trees so still they might as well have been carved
            in relief. The city

                    to the south cooks like only cement can.
            I think of sand. I think of sand this far from the ocean

                    and memorize
a simple sound before thinking of an image. Whatever I imagine,

2.

I find the next day in a bookstore gone dark, a rainy day,
        a book split open, its spine full of atmosphere.

             I was thinking about veins,

and now I remember my body torn open
        on the mast of night. The night before. Imagine:

        the only light in the house was from the TV.
And the weather simmers

            right along the Eastern Time Zone's seam.

        I have digressed
            from my original point. I wanted to say: the lawns

were so beautiful I could
        have slept on them. We nearly did. We nearly thought of doubt

            as a garment draped around the night. We nearly saw
        fishing line in the sky, but it turns out
it was just in the trees.

Goodbye to All That, the Birds Included

There are some other things in the painting
      that I didn't see the first time around.

The hull of a car. The trash scattered in the air.

      And scholars thought they were birds. I kind of did, too.
After all this time, goodbye

      to all that and this and that.
I hope the insects become magnetic,

      to eat plastic hillsides, to pull a drone down, even.

      It might even be a collage, now that I'm looking closer.
What does any of this even mean?
      What is there in the world that we do not say goodbye to?

      Goodbye to war? A scholar once said that war
makes us rhyme with each other. And music is the fluttering trash

in the collage or painting or whatever
      we want to call it. It is under glass so I place

my face up against the reflection and wait for it to pull me inside.

IV

Let us all be from somewhere.
Let us tell each other everything we can.

—Bob Hicok,
"A Primer"

Elegy for a Thousand Half-Masts

1.

If Saturday could be the Natural History of something—
      let's say plants

and be done with it. After all.
      After all this time the storm window still slaps
          against the house and the rainsong

      reminds me of digging
into someone

      with one word over and over
until that word becomes the root of all words, the manic starting point

      of sound and noise blending into each other, a soldier
walking through the woods

      and finding himself as a boy.

2.

If a metal barrel long cold. If a tree pointed to a sky

      I can only call declarative at this hour, at this moment:
a courageous landscape

      gone cold through the tight view of a camera lens,
a microscopic view of a life, abridged and abbreviated

        to a single moment
at the kitchen sink, a broken glass, feeling your heartbeat rise up and out,

      a fluttering

      not like a bird, but like a sentence of advice — who said it,
        you can't remember now — that if you

         must get drunk with the moon,
make sure it's a new moon

      so no one — not even yourself —
can see if you have become the reflection you dreamt yourself to be.

3.

Birds waiting past April to return —
　　　you looked outside.

You flipped a coin
　　　　　in your fingers in the pocket of your jacket

and you thought of — no — you yearned to be
　　　homesick

　　　　　as though restlessness were the only way
you could *feel* at home —

　　　　　for at home the icebox hums,
the heat dries out your eyes,

　　　the hard water of the shower
weighs you down —

　　　cracked driveway — narrative scripted,

unbroken:

4.

A spoon brandished at the sky, light reflected back at the sun,

       a fishbone for your thoughts, a fishbone for the throat
of memory. True, a throat's too likely to choke on a lie,

         a glass bottle buried in the garden —
slightly cracked — but reliability branches from vulnerability,

or at least that's what your mother said
         as she looked into the woods shrinking back
     from the porch light,
the symmetry only dreams are made of.

And *dipping here in this cultivated storm,*

         a cartographer whose map changes daily —
    it is only the wind,

       it is only the wind
that changes the landscape,

     the savage wind

takes you apart — a part of you — a memory, a map.

Light Bulb Hum

I see myself in the flicker
        and swell of burning out. The sound of a bridge

being rebuilt. A spark for good luck. A bridge
        on the other side of the world
                falls in on itself,

        and the neighbor's dog barks through the night.

                A quilt seen against the eyelids, a dark I know now
thanks to light. Little did I know at the beginning.

A thousand facts about the end
        of the world. A twenty-one gun salute. A glass of wine
                gripped tight, split open against the palm.

        I am sure my knees are well worn from praying beneath

an untreadable flag, a heavy offering plate I see in the sun.
        What more do we have to give? The dog barks on —

        the sparks above the new bridge fly,
and the weather above us listens to everything below far better

than we could have hoped for. When I think
        of a thousand years,

I think of nothing but sand and smoke, I think of a patient sadness
        that will out-wait the memory of a spark.

In Light of Recent Developments

We are not thinking of the president
        tonight. Even now, there is a maze cut into a cornfield

      not far from here.
The leaves pile up and we wait on the porch,

       we are waiting for the leaves
to self-combust and enter the air, the atmosphere, our lungs.

It's easy to mistake
      dust for smoke. It's easy to think of William Blake while the sun

burns a hole in my eyes. There is a certain labor I see in the sun,
      a type of hard work someone once

       warned me against — as if hard work and sweat
could wipe one from the face of the earth. Thinking
      of salt pork and a bridge

     fit for only one car at a time. A detailed aftermath.
     An aftermath usually is. Memory,
       like Blake, seems to change.

When I think of nature, nature thinks back.
      Or nature blinks back. The man with a stroller
filled with aluminum cans is now coming back up the street

     with a wheelbarrow. If that is what
    he had been saving for,
I wish I had carried a bag of cans out to him. I once thought

    expecting the worst was the best I could do.

Maybe Motion Will Save Us All

What matters is gravity.
      The newspaper lands

            on the front step, the words
rushing together, then parting again. Wishing for tomorrow's
            news today, I check

      the pages to see how the symbols add up
and where they lead. I find nothing. I wait for the mail
            and watch for the allegorical sky,

      the rain sweeping overhead, a lake blocking the sun,
            and think of the ark crashing against the waves,
the ark on dry land at last,

      and Noah: how his face must have turned away from clouds
            forever after.

I turn my head, close my eyes, and see years
of news in my mind — the way
an old film might turn and turn until
all that's left on the screen is a dull yellow light:

a hummingbird projector.

The children next door moving backward — back

inside to huddle around a TV that was broken, but now is not.
As they see it, the sun is a bruise on the sky.

A piece of rope around a tree seems

like the only way out, but if they
just keep going backward, their hunger

will fold in on itself, and all they will see
is that first moment of light, a brick tossed

over a bridge and into a river,
the splash unseen — but echoing and heard.

One Moment of Waking

When you are standing at the El, one in the morning,
            and the train
        going in the opposite direction stops for passengers,

the conductor will climb out with a flashlight
            and walk

        down the middle of the track,
as if looking for something caught in the wheels.
        And you will wonder how long

            you will wait for the next train, the one going toward the Loop,
                    the one with a man on it who will exit

            when the train stops for you.

        You will take a seat near a man
with no teeth

                who will move closer once the conductor is back
                    on the train

        and the man with a tunnel for a mouth will tell you how beautiful
your wife is and how this pocket full of change

                —he will hold it out to you: there is only one quarter—

with your help will take him to California.

And it will make you wonder if you were born
to sit on this train at this hour and listen

to this man's story as though it might one
day be your own, as if all autobiography — everyone's — is sleeping inside

this man, waiting to wake up. Because soon enough
he is sleeping, his hand
still outstretched, his hand still weaving stitches into the air.

And you will think how beautiful
your wife is. And you will think of everything

that has brought you to this moment

on the train. And you will think of how the train
is a metaphor for a river.

And you will think of a boat.

Reaching for a Lexicon, an Apple No Longer Shining

With my father contemplating the weather here,
      I am renaming everything in the kitchen,

everything that already has a name —
        except for the northern plains. Returning to weather,

           always returning to weather,
I suggest you read one word where you see another,

        but when one is busy
           renaming, there is only representation. And weather.
And recycling bins

        blowing up against the house, caught in the wind tunnel
of the driveway. No newspaper, no news. A simple sleep
        fell upon the city,

           upon the skin we all wear,
        upon the skin that grows waterproof even

           as we wish to become water.
The night is making like a tree

        and we are raking it all up holding it in our hands
           and you ask *O, what would we do if we didn't?* But asking

      masquerades as action,
        and the noise and the wind and the sound
of the night end up

      catalogued in memory. Through your eyes,

          I plan to watch myself grow obsolete. I plan to speak
the language of two hundred years ago.

How to Stop Migration

1.

Glad for the dust I am, for in its pattern
        I see an order beyond its name. Civility

              in the rain as well, window I wish to break,
        window I broke, all the same, repaired, broke again,

              the bees get used to the keeper — one of their own —
        and the sky
once wrapped in a rug

        did not turn out to be the same sky when unwrapped and revealed,
but how could I have known?

        Tell me
              how could I have known my body

would fit so well into a barrel, into the river, over the falls —

        how to stop migration —
five thousand doves, dyed black:

              a darkened sky —
        a voice says: Houdini would have worn three pairs of handcuffs,

a lead blindfold and —
        it's true —
              shaken them all off.

2.

What's more important than all of this,
        what's always been more important

than any of this, is the question

of how to set work aside for another day —
for instance,

every ninety seconds a grocery cart is stolen
but where, the voice asks, do they all go? The frontier

is a grand place, but a mountain of steel
and twisted metal

is grander, somehow, in the eaves of the mind — if only

for the strange beauty of it. But wait —

I do not mean to say
a pile of shopping carts can somehow overtake
what nature has always had a right to —

after all, I was once called a nature poet
by my mother

and nature weighs more
than all the shopping carts in the world —
though all of this is as peripheral to us

as only mass can be —
truly, all of this is to say:
step away from the tree you've been leaning against,

come with me, can you,
come with me to the top of these shopping carts

and look at the moon and tell me — please tell me —
is it not right now more beautiful than it's ever been?

A Hotel Lobby at the Edge of the World

1.

To spread your arms wide to a Michigan fall is to welcome
       what you are unsure of. Here, as with everywhere

              I have lived, there is a train,
there are train tracks, there is a sun, there are a hundred birds

              for every cloud,
a shared driveway, patches of dead grass, a broken window,

              and, as always, the heavy weight of air. A flag lifted early,
then lowered. A funeral, a citizen. A heavy balance.
              Can I tear the roof off

                     and spit far enough to hit an avenue?
              What I am leaving unsaid still hangs in the air.

What I am leaving behind is something no one is meant to bear.
                     Not a riptide.
              Not a nightfall. Not even a fly cast onto the water.

2.

I caught sight of the harbor between
        the buildings. I caught the sound of a helicopter

        spinning across the sky between
the buildings then gone. Shoulder to shoulder,

        the sidewalk, frightened. A light went out on the eighteenth floor.
Every day a shop closes early.

        Every day we fold a dozen obituaries on top of each other.

3.

There is a phone call
       for you in the lobby. In the lobby, a child is screaming

as if she has been crying since birth and nothing can stop her.
       There is no phone in the lobby.
There are a dozen people holding up their hands

       to show you where they live on the map.
            The lake, the thumb, the mitten. This might be an orchard

      of mistakes, but a tree turning in on itself is still a tree
and if someone gives you directions, you are bound
       to get lost. You are bound

      to find yourself one state over. A map
          when you close your eyes. A tree felled

      as if the fruit would never appear. You look
inside the trunk just to see how old it is and a starling flies

       from another bird's nest
     and somewhere, somewhere — maybe in the tree —
a phone *does* ring

and the concierge is standing next to you,
      the receiver waiting as always and you recall
your past, your future, but suddenly the baby

        is screaming for you to stop thinking,
    to pick up the phone, to say hello.

Adam Clay is the author of *The Wash*.
His poems have appeared in
Boston Review, Gulf Coast, Quarterly
West, Ploughshares, and elsewhere.
He co-edits *Typo Magazine* and lives in
Lexington, Kentucky with his family.

More Poetry from Milkweed Editions

To order books or for more information, contact Milkweed
at (800) 520-6455
or visit our Web site (www.milkweed.org).

Gaze
By Christopher Howell

The City, Our City
By Wayne Miller

What have you done to our ears to make us hear echoes?
By Arlene Kim

The Nine Senses
By Melissa Kwasny

Sharks in the Rivers
By Ada Limón

Fancy Beasts
By Alex Lemon

Milkweed Editions

Founded as a nonprofit organization in 1980, Milkweed Editions is an independent publisher. Our mission is to identify, nurture and publish transformative literature, and build an engaged community around it.

Join Us

In addition to revenue generated by the sales of books we publish, Milkweed Editions depends on the generosity of institutions and individuals like you. In an increasingly consolidated and bottom-line-driven publishing world, your support allows us to select and publish books on the basis of their literary quality and transformative potential. Please visit our Web site (www.milkweed.org) or contact us at (800) 520-6455 to learn more.

Milkweed Editions, a nonprofit publisher, gratefully acknowledges sustaining support from the following:

Maurice and Sally Blanks
Emilie and Henry Buchwald
The Bush Foundation
The Patrick and Aimee Butler
  Foundation
Timothy and Tara Clark
Betsy and Edward Cussler
The Dougherty Family Foundation
Julie B. DuBois
John and Joanne Gordon
Ellen Grace
William and Jeanne Grandy
John and Andrea Gulla
The Jerome Foundation
The Lerner Foundation
The Lindquist & Vennum
  Foundation
Sanders and Tasha Marvin
The McKnight Foundation
Mid-Continent Engineering
The Minnesota State Arts Board,
  through an appropriation by
  the Minnesota State Legislature
  and a grant from the National
  Endowment for the Arts
Kelly Morrison and John
  Willoughby
The National Endowment for
  the Arts
The Navarre Corporation
Ann and Doug Ness
Jörg and Angie Pierach

The RBC Foundation USA
Pete Rainey
Deborah Reynolds
Cheryl Ryland
Schele and Philip Smith
The Target Foundation
The Travelers Foundation
Moira and John Turner
Edward and Jenny Wahl

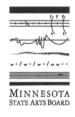

Interior design and typesetting by Hopkins/Baumann
Typeset in Bodoni
Printed on Recycled Cream 50# 440 PPI paper
by Edwards Brothers, Inc.